CAROLS FOR CHRISTMAS FROM ST PATRICK'S CATHEDRAL

CAROLS FOR

CHRISTMAS

✱ FROM ✱

ST PATRICK'S

CATHEDRAL

ARRANGED BY
JOHN DEXTER

CAROLS FOR CHRISTMAS

✳ FROM ✳
ST PATRICK'S CATHEDRAL

Carols arranged by

JOHN DEXTER

Organist and Master of the Choristers, St Patrick's Cathedral, Dublin

Introduction by

THE VERY REVEREND MAURICE STEWART

Dean of St Patrick's Cathedral

OLIVER
NELSON

THOMAS NELSON PUBLISHERS
Nashville • Atlanta • London • Vancouver

Designed by

THE BRIDGEWATER BOOK COMPANY LTD

Designed by Peter Bridgewater / Sarah Bentley

Published in Ireland by

Gill & Macmillan Ltd, Goldenbridge, Dublin 8

with associated companies throughout the world

Colour Library Books have used their best efforts to

trace all copyright holders. They will, however, make the usual

and appropriate arrangements with any who may have inadvertently

been overlooked and who contact them.

CLB 4268

Published in Nashville, Tennessee, by Thomas Nelson, Inc., Publishers,

and distributed in Canada by Word Communications, Ltd.,

Richmond, British Columbia.

ISBN 0–7852–7579–7

Printed in Singapore.

1 2 3 4 5 6 – 00 99 98 97 96 95

Front cover main:
ADORATION OF SHEPHERDS
Honthorst

Front cover panel and opposite title:
THE VIRGIN OF THE ROSARY
Murillo

Front cover detail:
DIPTYCH, ADORATION OF THE KINGS
Bruyn, The Elder

Endpapers:
THE ADORATION OF THE SHEPHERDS
Van Mander

Contents

Introduction

*N*o one knows for certain the origin of the Christmas carol, although the tradition can certainly be traced back for at least five hundred years. The carol today is an integral part of everybody's Christmas and it is hard to imagine the season of goodwill without it. We may hear it sung as part of the church service, or by warmly wrapped carollers fundraising for charity on our streets and doorsteps, or around the family piano. Wherever it is sung, the familiar phrases and harmonies bring back the remembered joys of Christmas past and remind us of the real meaning of this winter festival.

The St Patrick's Cathedral Carol Service has become an enormously popular part of Christmas, both for those attending it on Christmas Eve and for those futher afield listening to the radio. I am particularly delighted then to welcome this collection of Christmas carols compiled by the Cathedral's Master of the Choristers John Dexter. With almost twenty years of experience of organising the music for our carol service, there can be few people with as wide a knowledge of carols as John. From his hoard he has made this

ANGEL MUSICIAN
Melozzo da Forli 1438–1494

THE ADORATION *Gerolamo da Santacroce*

personal selection, mixing family favorites with the lesser known, to bring together in this exquisite book some of the most beautiful words and melodies of the Christian year.

The book is a timely reminder to us all that carols were written to be sung. In doing so we can all re-live the joy of the Christmas story.

Maurice Stewart

THE FEAST OF THE ROSE GARDENS
Albrecht Dürer 1471–1528

Adeste, Fideles

ANON.

WORDS LATIN, ANON. (18th CENT.)
ENGLISH TRANSLATION BY F. OAKELEY

1. A - de - ste, fi - de - les, Lae - ti, tri - um - phan - tes, Ve - ni - te, ve - ni - te in
1. O come, all ye faith - ful, Joy - ful and tri - um - phant, O come ye, O come ye to

Beth - le - hem! Na - tum vi - de - te Re - gem An - ge - lo - rum! *Ve - ni - te, a - do -*
Beth - le - hem! Come and be - hold him, Born the King of An - gels! O come, let us a -

- re - mus! Ve - ni - te, a - do - re - mus! Ve - ni - te, a - do - re - mus Do - mi - num!
- dore him! O come, let us a - dore him! O come, let us a - dore him, Christ the Lord!

2 God of God,
Light of Light,
Lo! he abhors not the Virgin's womb;
Very God,
Begotten, not created.

3 Sing, choirs of angels!
Sing in exultation!
Sing, all ye citizens of heaven above:
'Glory to God
In the highest.'

4 Yea, Lord, we greet thee,
Born this happy morning;
Jesu, to thee be glory given,
Word of the Father
Now in flesh appearing.

MUSICAL ANGEL WITH VIOLIN
Melozzo da Forli 1438–1494

ANGELS, FROM THE REALMS OF GLORY

FRENCH TRADITIONAL

WORDS BY J. MONTGOMERY

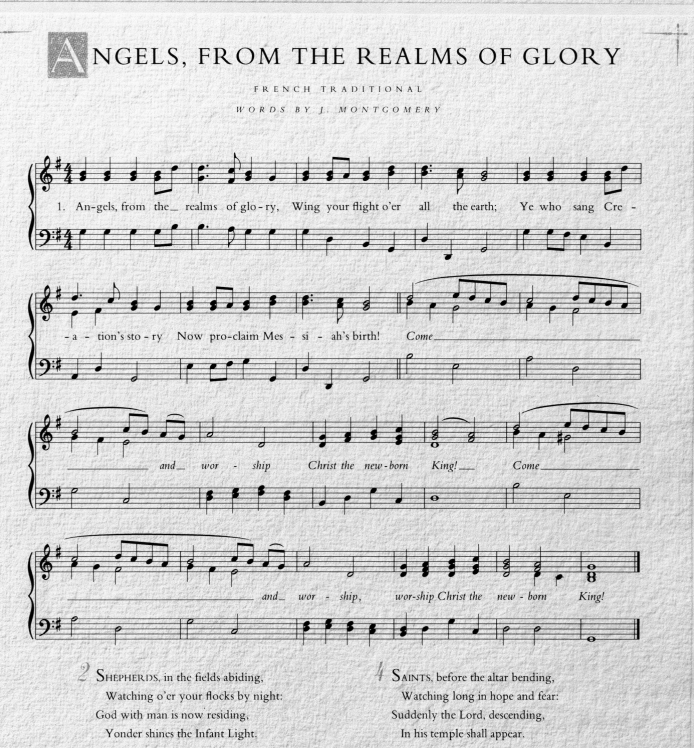

1. An-gels, from the realms of glo-ry, Wing your flight o'er all the earth; Ye who sang Cre-a-tion's sto-ry Now pro-claim Mes-si-ah's birth! Come and wor-ship Christ the new-born King! Come and wor-ship, wor-ship Christ the new-born King!

2 SHEPHERDS, in the fields abiding,
   Watching o'er your flocks by night:
God with man is now residing,
   Yonder shines the Infant Light.

3 SAGES, leave your contemplations:
   Brighter visions beam afar.
Seek the Great Desire of Nations:
   Ye have seen his natal star.

4 SAINTS, before the altar bending,
   Watching long in hope and fear:
Suddenly the Lord, descending,
   In his temple shall appear.

5 THOUGH an infant now we view him,
   He shall fill his Father's throne,
Gather all the nations to him;
   Every knee shall then bow down.

As with Gladness

W. H. MONK (FROM KOCHER)

WORDS BY W. C. DIX

1. As with gladness men of old Did the guiding star behold;

As with joy they hailed its light, Leading onward, beaming bright;

So, most gracious Lord, may we Evermore be led to thee.

2 As with joyful steps they sped,
Saviour, to thy lowly bed;
There to bend the knee before
Thee whom heaven and earth adore;
So may we with willing feet
Ever seek thy mercy-seat.

3 As they offered gifts most rare
At thy cradle rude and bare;
So may we with holy joy,
Pure and free from sin's alloy,
All our costliest treasures bring,
Christ, to thee, our heavenly King.

THE ADORATION OF THE MAGI
Giovanni B. Castello 1547–1637

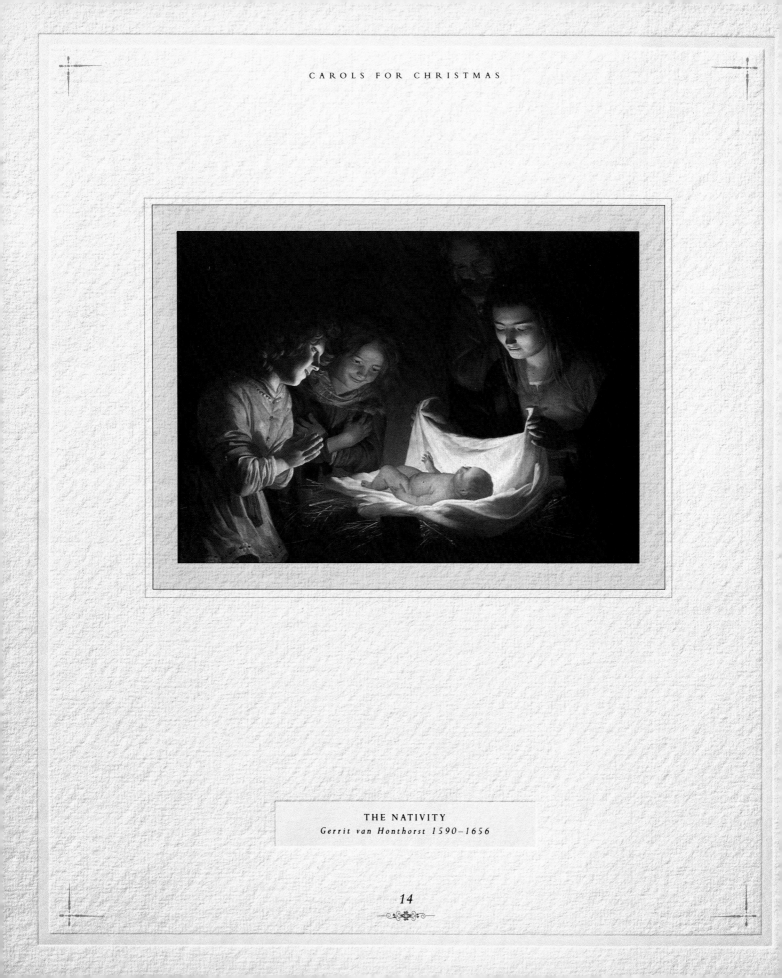

THE NATIVITY
Gerrit van Honthorst 1590–1656

WAY IN A MANGER

W. J. KIRKPATRICK
WORDS ANON.

1. A - way in a ___ man - ger, no ___ crib for a bed, The ___ lit - tle Lord

Je - sus laid ___ down his sweet head; The stars in the ___ bright sky looked

down where he lay The ___ lit - tle Lord Je - sus a - sleep on the hay.

2 THE cattle are lowing, the Baby awakes,
But little Lord Jesus, no crying he makes.
I love thee, Lord Jesus! look down from the sky,
And stay by my side until morning is nigh.

3 BE near me, Lord Jesus: I ask thee to stay
Close by me for ever, and love me I pray;
Bless all the dear children in thy tender care,
And take us to heaven to live with thee there.

DECK THE HALL

WELSH TRADITIONAL

WORDS ANON.

1. Deck the hall with boughs of hol-ly: Fa la la la la la la la la!
'Tis the sea-son to be jol-ly! Fa la la la la la la la la!
Fill the mead cup, drain the bar-rel, Fa la la la la la la la la!
Troll the an-cient Christ-mas ca-rol. Fa la la la la la la la la!

2 SEE the flowing bowl before us!
Strike the harp and join the chorus!
Follow me in merry measure,
While I sing of beauty's treasure.

3 FAST away the old year passes,
Hail the new, ye lads and lasses!
Laughing, quaffing, all together,
Heedless of the wind and weather.

DECORATING WITH HOLLY
John Callcott Horsley 1817–1903

DIA DO BHEATH'

IRISH TRADITIONAL

WORDS BY AODH MAC CATHMHAOIL

1. Dia do bheath' a naoidhe naoimh, 'Sa mhainséar cé____ bocht____ Meidhreach____ saibhir a tá tú____ Glórmhar id' dhún féin anocht.

1. All hail and welcome holy child, You poor babe in the manger. So happy and rich it is you are Tonight__ inside__ your castle.

2 DIA do bheath' a Íosa 'rís!
   'Do bheatha, i gclí an Óigh!
   A Ghnúis is áille ná'n ghrian,
   Na mílte fáilte do Dhia óg!

3 GOD bless you, Jesu, once again!
   Your life in its young body,
   Your face more lovely than the sun
   A thousand welcomes, Baby!

4 MÍLE fáilte 'nocht i gclí
   Le mo chroíse dom Rí fial,
   I ndá nádur do chuaigh, póg
   Is fáilte uaim do Dhia!

5 TONIGHT we greet you in the flesh;
   My heart adores my young King.
   You came to us in human form
   I bring you a kiss and a greeting.

ADORATION OF THE SHEPHERDS
Fray Juan Bautista Maino (Mayno) 1578–1649

NATIVITY
Charles Poerson 1609–1667

DING DONG! MERRILY

T. ARBEAU

WORDS BY G. R. WOODWARD

1. Ding dong! mer - ri - ly on high In heaven the bells are ring - ing:

Ding dong! ve - ri - ly the sky Is riv'n with an - gel sing - ing:

Glo - - - - - -

- - ri - a! Ho - san - na in ex - cel - sis!

2 E'EN so here below, below;
Let steeple bells be swungen.
And *iö, iö, iö,*
By priests and people sungen:

3 PRAY you dutifully prime
Your Matin chime, ye ringers;
May you beautifully rime
Your Eve-time song, ye singers:

GOD REST YOU MERRY, GENTLEMEN

ENGLISH TRADITIONAL

WORDS·ENGLISH·TRADITIONAL

1. God rest you mer - ry, gen - tle - men, Let no - thing you dis - may, For

Je - sus Christ our Sa - viour Was born up - on this day, To save us all from

Sa - tan's power When we had gone a - stray: O____ ti - dings of com - fort and

joy! Com-fort and joy! O____ ti - dings of com - fort and joy!

2 FROM God our Heavenly Father
   A blessèd angel came;
  And unto certain shepherds
   Brought tidings of the same;
  How that in Bethlehem was born
   The Son of God by name:

3 NOW to the Lord sing praises,
   All you within this place;
  And with true love and brotherhood
   Each other now embrace.
  This holy tide of Christmas
   All others doth efface:

ANGEL MUSICIAN
Melozzo da Forli 1438–1494

GOOD CHRISTIAN MEN REJOICE

ANON. (13th CENT.)

WORDS BY J. M. NEALE

1. Good Christ - ian men, re - joice_____ With heart and soul and voice!_____ Give ye heed to what we say: News! news! Je - sus Christ is born to - day! Ox and ass be - fore him bow, And he is in the man - ger now: Christ is born to - day!_____ Christ is born to - day!

2 GOOD Christian men, rejoice
With heart and soul and voice!
Now ye hear of endless bliss:
Joy! joy!
Jesus Christ was born for this!
He hath oped the heavenly door,
And man is blessèd evermore:
Christ was born for this!

3 GOOD Christian men, rejoice
With heart and soul and voice!
Now ye need not fear the grave:
Peace! peace!
Jesus Christ was born to save!
Calls you one and calls you all,
To gain his everlasting hall:
Christ was born to save!

MYSTIC NATIVITY
Sandro Botticelli c.1445–1510

**HABITANTS RETURNING WITH SUPPLIES
BY MOONLIGHT**
Cornelius Krieghoff 1815–1872

GOOD KING WENCESLAS

ANON. (14th CENT.)

WORDS BY J. M. NEALE

1. Good King Wen-ces - las looked out   On the feast of   Ste - phen,   When the snow lay   round a-bout,

Deep and crisp and   e - ven;   Bright-ly shone the   moon that night,   Though the frost was

- cru - el,   When a   poor man   came in sight,   Gath-'ring win - ter   fu   –   el.

2 'HITHER, page, and stand by me;
   If thou know'st it, telling –
Yonder peasant, who is he?
   Where and what his dwelling?'
'Sire, he lives a good league hence,
   Underneath the mountain,
Right against the forest fence,
   By Saint Agnes' fountain.'

3 'BRING me flesh and bring me wine!
   Bring me pine logs hither!
Thou and I will see him dine
   When we bear them thither.'
Page and monarch forth they went,
   Forth they went together,
Through the rude wind's wild lament
   And the bitter weather.

4 'SIRE, the night is darker now,
   And the wind blows stronger;
Fails my heart, I know not how,
   I can go no longer.'
'Mark my footsteps, good my page,
   Tread thou in them boldly:
Thou shalt find the winter's rage
   Freeze thy blood less coldly.'

5 IN his master's steps he trod,
   Where the snow lay dinted;
Heat was in the very sod
   Which the saint had printed.
Therefore, Christian men, be sure,
   Wealth or rank possessing,
Ye who now will bless the poor
   Shall yourselves find blessing.

OOD PEOPLE ALL

IRISH TRADITIONAL

WORDS IRISH AND ENGLISH TRADITIONAL

1. Good peo-ple_ all, this Christ-mas time, Con-si-der well_ and bear in mind What our good God for us has done, In send-ing his_ be-lo-vèd Son. With Ma-ry ho-ly we should pray To_ God_ with love_ this Christ-mas Day; In Beth-le-hem up-on that morn There was a bless-èd Mes-si-ah born.

2 THE night before the happy tide
  The noble Virgin and her guide
  Were long time seeking up and down
  To find a lodging in the town.
  But hark how all things come to pass:
  From every door repelled, alas!
  As long foretold, their refuge all
  Was but an humble ox's stall.

3 NEAR Bethlehem did shepherds keep
  Their flocks of lambs and feeding sheep;
  To whom God's angels did appear,
  Which put the shepherds in great fear.
  'Prepare and go', the angels said,
  'To Bethlehem; be not afraid,
  For there you'll find this happy morn,
  A princely Babe, sweet Jesus, born.'

THE BIRTH OF CHRIST
Master to James IV of Scotland
16th century

CONCERT OF ANGELS, NATIVITY
Grünewald c.1470/80–1528

HARK! THE HERALD-ANGELS SING

MENDELSSOHN

WORDS BY C. WESLEY

1. Hark! the her-ald-an-gels sing!_ Glo-ry to the new-born King; Peace on earth, and mer-cy mild,_ God and sin-ners re-con-ciled! Joy-ful, all ye na-tions, rise,_ Join the tri-umph of the skies;_ With th'an-gel-ic host pro-claim, Christ is_ born in Beth-le-hem. *Hark! the he-rald-an-gels sing!* Glo-ry_ to the new-born King.

2 CHRIST, by highest heaven adored!
Christ, the everlasting Lord!
Late in time behold him come,
Offspring of a Virgin's womb.
Veiled in flesh the Godhead see;
Hail, the incarnate Deity,
Pleased as Man with men to dwell,
Jesus, our Emmanuel.

3 HAIL, the heaven-born Prince of peace!
Hail, the Sun of righteousness!
Light and life to all he brings,
Risen with healing in his wings.
Mild, he lays his glory by,
Born that man no more may die,
Born to raise the sons of earth,
Born to give them second birth.

VIRGIN AND CHILD WITH
INFANT ST JOHN THE BAPTIST
Balthasar Beschey 1708–1776

I KNOW A ROSE-TREE

PRAETORIUS

WORDS ANON. (15th CENT. GERMAN)

1. I know a rose-tree spring - ing Forth from an an - cient root. As men of old were sing - ing From Jes - se came the shoot That bore a blos-som bright A - mid the cold of win - ter When half spent was the night.

2 THIS rose-tree, blossom-laden,
Whereof Isaiah spake,
Is Mary, peerless maiden,
Who mothered, for our sake,
The little Child, new-born
By God's eternal counsel
On that first Christmas morn.

3 O FLOWER, whose fragrance tender
With sweetness fills the air,
Dispel in glorious splendour
The darkness ev'rywhere;
True man, yet very God,
From sin and death now save us,
And share our every load.

ADORATION OF THE SHEPHERDS
Domenico Ghirlandaio 1449–1494

I LOOK FROM AFAR

PLAINCHANT

I look__ from a - far and lo, I see the power of God coming and a cloud covering the whole earth.__

Go ye out to meet him and__ say, Tell us, art thou he that should come to reign over thy peo-ple Is - ra - el?__

High and low,__ rich and poor; one with an - oth - er,___ Go ye out to meet him and__ say,

Hear O thou shepherd of Israel, thou that leadest Jo-seph like a sheep, Tell us, art thou he that should come?

Stir up thy strength O Lord, And come__ to reign over thy peo - ple Is - ra - el.___

Glory be to the Fa - ther and to the Son; and to the Ho - ly Ghost. I look__ from a - far

and lo, I see the power of God coming, and a cloud covering the whole earth.___

Go ye out to meet him and__ say, Tell us, art thou he that should come to reign over thy peo-ple Is - ra - el?__

ADORATION OF THE SHEPHERDS
Palma Vecchio 1480 - 1528

IN DULCI JUBILO

ANON. (13th CENT.)

WORDS ANON. (14th CENT.) GERMAN

1. In dul - ci ju - bi - lo_____ Let us our hom - age shew;_____
Our hearts' joy re - cli - neth In prae - se - pi - o_____ And
like a bright star shi - neth, Ma - tris in gre - mi - o._____
Al - pha es et O,_____ Al - pha es et O.

2 *O* JESU *parvule!*
I yearn for thee alway!
Hear me, I beseech thee,
O Puer optime!
My prayer let it reach thee,
O Princeps gloriæ!
Trahe me post te!

3 *O* PATRIS *caritas*
O Nati lenitas!
Deeply were we stained
Per nostra crimina;
But thou hast for us gained
Coelorum gaudia.
O that we were there.

4 *U*BI *sunt gaudia,*
If that they be not there?
There are angels singing,
Nova cantica,
There the bells are ringing
In Regis curia:
O that we were there.

INFANT HOLY

POLISH · TRADITIONAL

WORDS POLISH TRADITIONAL, TRANSLATED BY E. REED

1. In - fant ho - ly, In - fant low - ly, For his bed a cat - tle stall; Ox - en low - ing, lit - tle know - ing Christ the Babe is Lord of all. Swift - ly wing - ing an - gels sing - ing, No-wells ring - ing, ti - dings bring - ing: Christ the Babe is Lord of all.

2 FLOCKS were sleeping, shepherds keeping
    Vigil till the morning new;
Saw the glory, heard the story,
    Tidings of a gospel true.
Thus rejoicing, free from sorrow,
    Praises voicing, greet the morrow:
Christ the Babe was born for you.

THE HOURS OF ETIENNE CHEVALIER
Jean Fouquet c.1425–1480

IN THE BLEAK MIDWINTER

HOLST

WORDS BY C. ROSSETTI

1. In the bleak mid-win-ter, Frost-y wind made moan, Earth stood hard as ir-on, Wa-ter like a stone: Snow had fall-en, snow on snow, Snow on snow, In the bleak mid-win-ter, Long a-go.

2 Our God, heaven cannot hold him,
Nor earth sustain:
Heaven and earth shall flee away
When he comes to reign:
In the bleak mid-winter
A stable place sufficed
The Lord God almighty
Jesus Christ.

3 Enough for him, whom Cherubim
Worship night and day,
A breastful of milk
And a manger full of hay:
Enough for him, whom angels
Fall down before,
The ox and ass and camel
Which adore.

4 What can I give him,
Poor as I am?
If I were a shepherd
I would bring a lamb;
If I were a wise man
I would do my part;
Yet what I can I give him
Give my heart.

ADORATION OF THE MAGI
Pieter II Bruegel c.1564–1638

THE MADONNA AND CHILD IN GLORY
Sassoferrato 1609–1685

I SAW THREE SHIPS

ENGLISH TRADITIONAL

WORDS ENGLISH TRADITIONAL

1. I saw three ships come sail-ing in On Christ-mas Day, on Christ-mas Day, I saw three ships come sail-ing in On Christ-mas Day in the morn-ing.

2 AND what was in those ships all three?

3 OUR Saviour Christ and his lady,

4 PRAY, whither sailed those ships all three?

5 O THEY sailed into Bethlehem

6 AND all the bells on earth shall ring

7 AND all the angels in heaven shall sing

8 AND all the souls on earth shall sing

9 THEN let us all rejoice amain!

It Came Upon the Midnight Clear

SULLIVAN (FROM AN ENGLISH TRADITIONAL MELODY)

WORDS BY E. H. SEARS

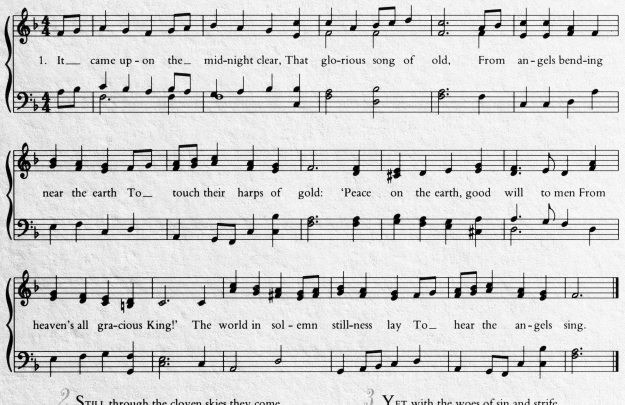

1. It__ came up-on the__ mid-night clear, That glo-rious song of old, From an-gels bend-ing near the earth To__ touch their harps of gold: 'Peace on the earth, good will to men From heaven's all gra-cious King!' The world in sol-emn still-ness lay To__ hear the an-gels sing.

2 STILL through the cloven skies they come
  With peaceful wings unfurled;
And still their heavenly music floats
  O'er all the weary world;
Above its sad and lowly plains
  They bend on hovering wing,
And ever o'er its Babel-sounds
  The blessèd angels sing.

3 YET with the woes of sin and strife
  The world has suffered long;
Beneath the angel-strain have rolled
  Two thousand years of wrong;
And man, at war with man, hears not
  The words of peace they bring:
O listen now, ye men of strife,
  And hear the angels sing!

4 FOR lo! the days are hastening on,
  By prophet-bards foretold,
When, with the ever-circling years,
  Comes round the age of gold:
When peace shall over all the earth
  Its ancient splendours fling,
And the whole world give back the song
  Which now the angels sing.

THE BIRTH OF CHRIST
Giotto c.1266–1337

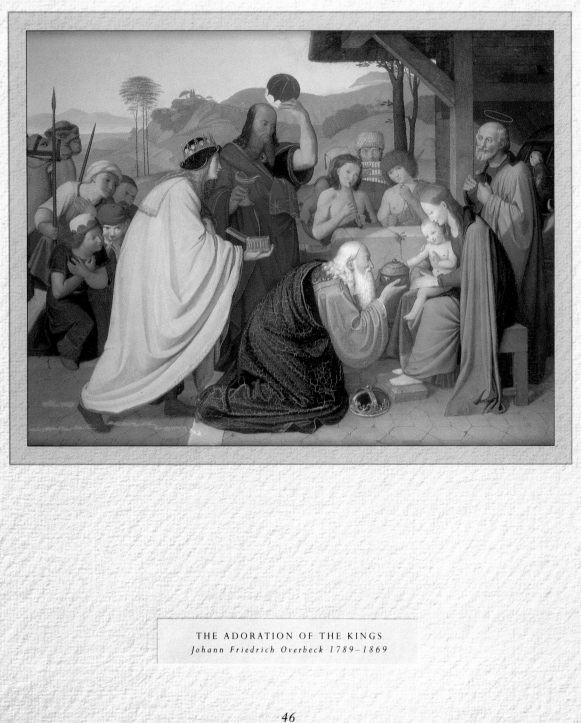

THE ADORATION OF THE KINGS
Johann Friedrich Overbeck 1789–1869

JOY TO THE WORLD

ANON.

WORDS BY I. WATTS

1. Joy to the world! the Lord is come: Let earth re-ceive her King! Let ev'-ry heart pre-pare him room, And heav'n and na-ture sing, And heav'n and na-ture sing, And heav'n, and heav'n and na-ture sing!

2 Joy to the earth! the Saviour reigns:
Let men their songs employ,
While fields and floods, rocks, hills and plains
Repeat the sounding joy.

3 He rules the world with truth and grace,
And makes the nations prove
The glories of his righteousness
And wonders of his love.

OVE CAME DOWN AT CHRISTMAS

IRISH TRADITIONAL

WORDS BY C. ROSSETTI

1. Love came down at Christ - mas, Love all love - ly,__ Love di - vine;__

Love was born at Christ - mas, Star and an - gels__ gave the sign.

2 WORSHIP we the Godhead,
    Love incarnate, Love divine;
Worship we our Jesus:
    But wherewith for sacred sign?

3 LOVE shall be our token,
    Love be yours and love be mine,
Love to God and all men,
    Love for plea and gift and sign.

HOLY FAMILY
Raphael 1483–1520

LULLY LULLA

ANON. (16th CENT.)

WORDS ANON. (16th CENT.)

Lul - ly lul - la, thou lit - tle ti - ny child, By by, lul - ly lul - lay. 1. O sis - ters too, How may we do For to pre - serve this day This poor young - ling, For whom we do sing, By by, lul - ly lul - lay?

2 HEROD the king,
In his raging,
Charged he hath this day
His men of might,
In his own sight,
All young children to slay.

3 THAT woe is me,
Poor child for thee!
And ever morn and day,
For thy parting
Neither say nor sing
By by, lully lullay!

TWO ANGELS
Charles François Sellier 1830–1882

THE VISITATION
From Le Livre d'Heures du Maréchal Boucicaut
early 15th century

O COME, O COME EMMANUEL

ANON.

WORDS TRANSLATED FROM LATIN ANTIPHON BY J. M. NEALE

1. O come, O come Em - ma - nu - el, And ran-som cap-tive Is - ra - el, That

mourns in lone - ly ex - ile here. Un - til the Son of God____ ap - pear: Re -

-joice! Re - joice! Em - ma - nu - el Shall come to thee, O Is - ra - el.

2 O COME, thou Rod of Jesse, free
Thine own from Satan's tyranny;
From depths of hell thy people save,
And give them victory o'er the grave:

3 O COME, thou Day-spring, come and cheer
Our spirits by thine advent here;
Disperse the gloomy clouds of night,
And death's dark shadows put to flight:

4 O COME, thou Key of David, come
And open wide our heavenly home:
Make safe the way that leads on high,
And close the path to misery:

O HOLY NIGHT

A. ADAM

WORDS BY J. S. DWIGHT

1. O ho - ly night! the stars are bright - ly shi - ning, It is the night of the dear Sa - viour's birth; Long lay the world in sin and er - ror pi - ning, Till he ap-peared, and the soul felt its worth. A thrill of hope, the wea - ry world re - joi - ces, For

ADORATION OF THE KINGS
Roger van der Weyden 1399/1400–1464

LITTLE TOWN OF BETHLEHEM

ENGLISH TRADITIONAL

WORDS BY P. BROOKS

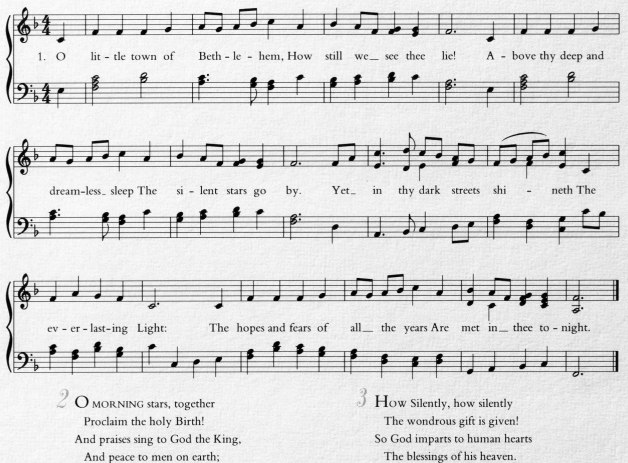

1. O lit-tle town of Beth-le-hem, How still we_ see thee lie! A-bove thy deep and dream-less_ sleep The si-lent stars go by. Yet_ in thy dark streets shi – neth The ev-er-last-ing Light: The hopes and fears of all_ the years Are met in_ thee to-night.

2 O MORNING stars, together
  Proclaim the holy Birth!
And praises sing to God the King,
  And peace to men on earth;
For Christ is born of Mary,
  And, gathered all above,
While mortals sleep, the angels keep
  Their watch of wondering love.

3 How Silently, how silently
  The wondrous gift is given!
So God imparts to human hearts
  The blessings of his heaven.
No ear may hear his coming,
  But, in this world of sin,
Where meek souls will receive him, still
  The dear Christ enters in.

4 O HOLY child of Bethlehem,
  Descend to us we pray;
Cast out our sin, and enter in:
  Be born in us today!
We hear the Christmas angels
  The great glad tidings tell;
O come to us, abide with us,
  Our Lord Emmanuel!

ONCE IN ROYAL DAVID'S CITY

H. J. GAUNTLETT

WORDS BY MRS C. F. ALEXANDER

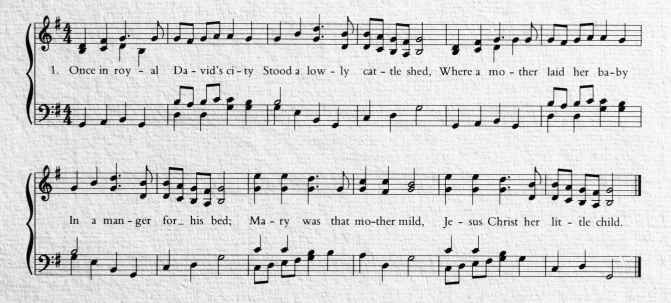

1. Once in roy - al Da - vid's ci - ty Stood a low - ly cat - tle shed, Where a mo - ther laid her ba - by

In a man - ger for his bed; Ma - ry was that mo - ther mild, Je - sus Christ her lit - tle child.

2 HE came down to earth from heaven
Who is God and Lord of all,
And his shelter was a stable,
And his cradle was a stall;
With the poor and mean and lowly
Lived on earth our Saviour holy.

3 AND through all his wondrous childhood,
He would honour and obey,
Love and watch the lowly mother
In whose gentle arms he lay:
Christian children all must be
Mild, obedient, good as he.

4 FOR he is our childhood's pattern,
Day by day, like us, he grew;
He was little, weak and helpless,
Tears and smiles like us he knew;
And he feeleth for our sadness,
And he shareth in our gladness.

5 AND our eyes at last shall see him,
Through his own redeeming love,
For that Child so dear and gentle
Is our Lord in heaven above;
And he leads his children on
To the place where he is gone.

6 NOT in that poor lowly stable,
With the oxen standing by,
We shall see him; but in heaven,
Set at God's right hand on high;
When like stars his children crowned
All in white shall wait around.

HOLY NIGHT
Carlo Maratta 1625–1713

ON CHRISTMAS NIGHT

ENGLISH TRADITIONAL

WORDS ENGLISH TRADITIONAL

1. On Christ-mas night all Christ-ians sing, To hear the news_ the an - gels bring. On
Christ-mas night all Christ-ians sing, To hear the news the an - gels bring. News of great
joy,_ news of __ great mirth, News of our mer - ci - ful_ King's birth.__

2 THEN why should men on earth be so sad,
Since our Redeemer made us glad,
When from our sin he set us free,
All for to gain our liberty.

3 WHEN sin departs before his grace,
Then life and health come in its place;
Angels and men with joy may sing,
All for to see the new-born King.

4 ALL out of darkness we have light,
Which made the angels sing this night;
'Glory to God and peace to men,
Now and for evermore. Amen.'

AN ANGEL
John Melhuish Strudwick 1849–1935

THE ADORATION OF THE CHILD WITH
ST JOHN THE BAPTIST AND ST ROMAULD
Fra Filippo Lippi c.1406–1469

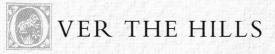VER THE HILLS

NORWEGIAN TRADITIONAL

WORDS BY M. C. GILLINGTON

1. O - ver the hills and__ o - ver the vales, O - ver the fields of snow, The
Christ - Child came and__ brought for me A gol - den__ shi - ning__ Christ-mas tree
It was a Cross, where - on did grow All hap-py things the__ world can know.

2 OVER the hills and over the vales,
Over the fields of snow,
The Christ-Child came and brought for me
A little bed so fair to see
It was a manger poor and bare,
But sweet and holy thoughts were there.

3 OVER the hills and over the vales,
Over the fields of snow,
The Christ-Child came and brought for me
A Christmas gift, the best might be:
O beauteous gift! It was the Love
That brought him here from heaven above.

4 OVER the hills and over the vales,
Over the fields of snow,
The Christ-Child wanders for my sake
And there will I my pathway take,
And there unto my Lord and King
My heart and worship will I bring.

REJOICE AND BE MERRY

ENGLISH TRADITIONAL

WORDS ENGLISH TRADITIONAL

1. Re - joice and be mer - ry in songs and in mirth; O praise our Re -
deem - er, all mor - tals on earth! For this is the birth - day of
Je - sus our King, Who brought us sal - va - tion: his prais - es we'll sing.

2 A HEAVENLY vision appeared in the sky;
Vast numbers of angels the shepherds did spy,
Proclaiming the birthday of Jesus our King,
Who brought us salvation: his praises we'll sing.

3 LIKEWISE a bright star in the sky did appear,
Which led the wise men from the East to draw near;
They found the Messiah, sweet Jesus our King.
Who brought us salvation: his praises we'll sing.

4 AND when they were come, they their treasures unfold,
And unto him offered myrrh, incense and gold.
So blessèd for ever be Jesus our King,
Who brought us salvation: his praises we'll sing.

ANGEL
Sir Edward Burne-Jones 1833–1898

THE ADORATION OF THE MAGI
Frans Francken the Elder 1542–1616

SEE AMID THE WINTER'S SNOW

J. GOSS

WORDS BY E. CASWALL

1. See, a-mid the win-ter's snow, Born for us on earth be-low, See, the ten-der Lamb ap-pears, Pro-mised from e-ter-nal years! *Hail, thou ev-er bless-èd morn! Hail, Re-demp-tion's* hap-py dawn! Sing through all Je-ru-sa-lem: 'Christ is born in Beth-le-hem!'

2 Lo! within a manger lies
  He who built the starry skies,
  He who, throned in height sublime,
  Sits amid the Cherubim.

3 Say, ye holy shepherds, say:
  What your joyful news today?
  Wherefore have ye left your sheep
  On the lonely mountain steep?

4 'As we watched at dead of night,
  Lo! we saw a wondrous light;
  Angels, singing 'Peace on earth',
  Told us of the Saviour's birth.'

5 Sacred Infant, all-divine,
  What a tender love was thine
  Thus to come from highest bliss
  Down to such a world as this!

6 Teach, oh teach us, holy Child,
  By thy face so meek and mild,
  Teach us to resemble thee
  In thy sweet humility!

SILENT NIGHT

F. X. GRUBER

WORDS: GERMAN, J. MOHR. IRISH TRANSLATION, T. O DONNCHADHA.
ENGLISH TRANSLATION, ANON.

1. Silent night, holy night, All is calm, all is bright, Round yon virgin mother and child, Holy infant so tender and mild, Sleep in heavenly peace, Sleep in heavenly peace.

2 Oíche chiún, oíche Mhic Dé;
Cách 'na suan, dís araon,
Dís is dílse 'faire le spéis,
Naíon beag gnaoigheal ceannann tais caomh:
Críost 'na chodladh go séimh.

3 Stille Nacht! Heilige Nacht!
Alles Schläft; einsam wacht
Nur das traute hoch heilige Paar
Holder Knabe im lockigen Haar,
Schlaf' im himmlischer Ruh!

NATIVITY SCENE
Georges de la Tour 1593–1652

ADORATION OF THE SHEPHERDS
Gerrit van Honthorst 1590–1656

SING A SWEET SONG

ENGLISH TRADITIONAL

WORDS BY C. E. PATTON

1. Sing a sweet song of Beth-le-hem ci-ty, Ca-rol to praise the Babe new-ly born; Ma-ry shall won-der, Ma-ry shall pon-der, An-gels shall sing this glad Christ-mas morn; Christ in his love, his love and his pi-ty Stoops down to save poor sin-ners for-lorn:

Slower and softer

Ring out glad bells, ring out the sweet sto - ry.

2 ANGELS shall sing in glorious measures,
   Shepherds shall haste and humbly draw near;
Mary shall wonder, Mary shall ponder
   All that is told by prophet and seer.
Sages, bring gifts, and open your treasures,
   Here is our hope: our Saviour is here.

ECCE ANCILLA DOMINI
Edward A. Fellowes-Prynne 1854–1921

THE ANGEL GABRIEL

BASQUE TRADITIONAL

WORDS BASQUE TRADITIONAL, TRANSLATED BY S. BARING-GOULD

1. The an-gel Ga-bri-el from hea-ven came,____ His wings as drift-ed snow, his eyes____ as flame:____ 'All hail,' said he, 'thou low-ly maid-en Ma-ry,____ *Most* high-ly fa-voured la-dy!' *Glo - ri - a!*____

2 'FOR known a blessed Mother thou shalt be;
   All generations laud and honour thee:
   Thy son shall be Emmanuel, by seers foretold.'

3 THEN gentle Mary meekly bowed her head;
   'To me be as it pleaseth God!' she said,
   'My soul shall laud and magnify his holy Name.'

4 OF her Emmanuel, the Christ, was born,
   In Bethlehem, all on a Christmas morn;
   And Christian folk throughout the world will ever say:

THE FIRST NOWELL

ENGLISH TRADITIONAL

WORDS ENGLISH TRADITIONAL

1. The first No-well the an-gel did say Was to cer-tain poor shep-herds in fields as they lay;
In fields where they lay keep-ing their sheep On a cold win-ter's night that was so deep:
No - well, No - well, No - well, No - well, Born is the King of Is - ra - el.

2 THEY lookèd up and saw a star
Shining in the east beyond them far,
And to the earth it gave great light,
And so it continued both day and night:

3 AND by the light of that same star,
Three wise men came from country far;
To seek for a king was their intent,
And to follow the star wherever it went:

4 THIS star drew nigh to the north-west,
O'er Bethlehem it took its rest,
And there it did both stop and stay
Right over the place where Jesus lay:

5 THEN entered in those wise men three,
Most reverently upon their knee,
And offered there in his presence,
Both gold, and myrrh, and frankincense:

6 THEN let us all with one accord
Sing praises to our heavenly Lord,
That hath made heaven and earth of nought,
And with his blood mankind hath bought:

ANNUNCIATION TO THE SHEPHERDS
Book of Hours, early 15th century

THE MADONNA AND CHILD
Julius Schnorr von Carolsfeld 1794–1872

THE HOLLY AND THE IVY

ENGLISH TRADITIONAL

WORDS ENGLISH TRADITIONAL

1. The hol-ly and the i-vy, When they are both full grown, Of__ all the trees that are in the wood, The__ hol-ly bears the crown. The ris-ing of the sun__ And the run-ning of the deer. The__ play-ing of the mer-ry or-gan, Sweet__ sing-ing in the choir.

2 THE holly bears a blossom
As white as the lily flower,
And Mary bore sweet Jesus Christ
To be our sweet Saviour.

3 THE holly bears a berry
As red as any blood,
And Mary bore sweet Jesus Christ
To do poor sinners good.

4 THE holly bears a prickle
As sharp as any thorn
And Mary bore sweet Jesus Christ
On Christmas Day in the morn.

5 THE holly bears a bark
As bitter as any gall,
And Mary bore sweet Jesus Christ
For to redeem us all.

BIRTH OF CHRIST
Melchior Broederlam
active c.1381–d.1409 or later

UNTO US IS BORN A SON

ANON. (14th CENT.)

WORDS ANON. TRANSLATED BY G. R. WOODWARD

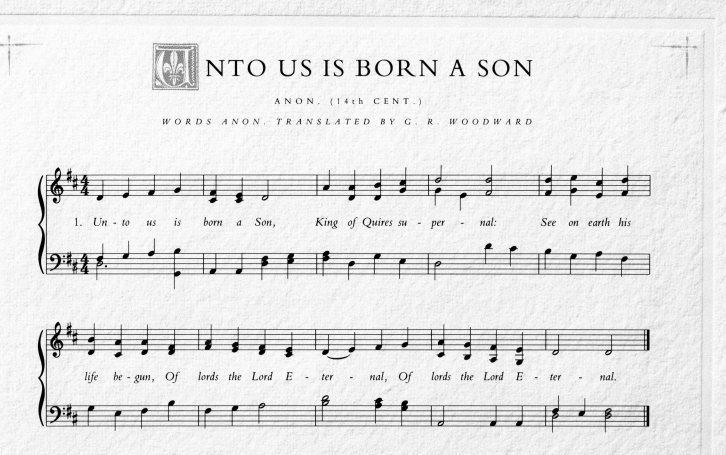

1. Un-to us is born a Son, King of Quires su-per-nal: See on earth his life be-gun, Of lords the Lord E-ter-nal, Of lords the Lord E-ter-nal.

2 CHRIST from heav'n descending low,
   Comes on earth a stranger;
   Ox and ass their owner know
   Becradled in a manger:

3 THIS did Herod sore affray,
   And grievously bewilder;
   So he gave the word to slay,
   And slew the little childer:

4 OF his love and mercy mild
   This is the Christmas story;
   And O that Mary's gentle Child
   Might lead us up to glory!

WE THREE KINGS

J. H. HOPKINS

WORDS BY J. H. HOPKINS

1. We three kings of O-ri-ent are, Bear-ing gifts we tra-verse a-far, Field and foun-tain, moor and moun-tain, Fol-low-ing yon-der star.

O_____ Star of Won-der, Star of Night, Star with roy-al beau-ty bright, West-ward lead-ing, still pro-ceed-ing, Guide us to thy per-fect light.

2 BORN a king on Bethlehem plain,
Gold I bring to crown him again,
King for ever, ceasing never
Over us all to reign.

3 FRANKINCENSE to offer have I,
Incense owns a Deity nigh;
Prayer and praising all men raising,
Worship him, God on high.

4 MYRRH is mine; its bitter perfume
Breathes a life of gathering gloom;
Sorrowing, sighing, bleeding, dying,
Sealed in a stone-cold tomb.

5 GLORIOUS now behold him arise,
King, and God, and sacrifice.
Heaven sing: 'Alleluia';
'Alleluia' the earth replies.

THE MEETING OF THE MAGI
*From Très Riches Heures du Duc de Berry
early 15th century*

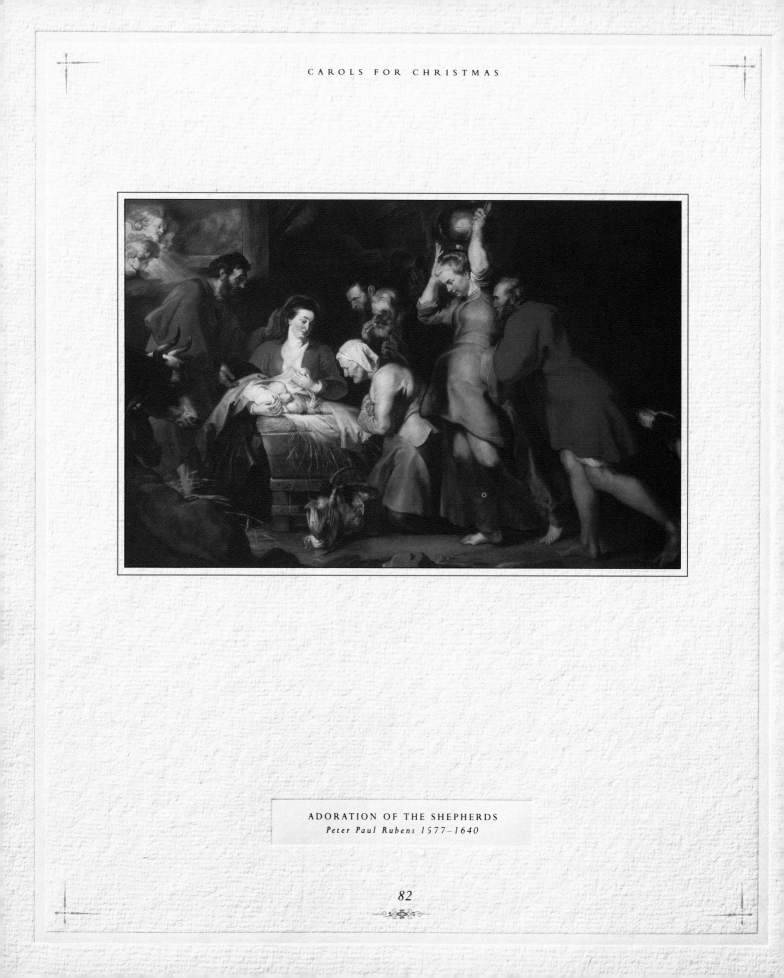

ADORATION OF THE SHEPHERDS
Peter Paul Rubens 1577–1640

WHAT CHILD IS THIS

ENGLISH TRADITIONAL

WORDS BY W. C. DIX

1. What Child is this, who laid to rest, On Ma-ry's lap is sleep-ing? Whom an-gels greet with an-thems sweet, While shep-herds watch are keep - ing?

This, this is Christ the King, Whom shep-herds guard and an-gels sing:

Haste, haste to bring him laud, The babe, the son of Ma - ry!

2 WHY lies he in such a mean estate,
   Where ox and ass are feeding?
   Good Christian, fear: for sinners here
   The silent Word is pleading:
   Nails, spear, shall pierce him through,
   The Cross be borne, for me, for you:
   Hail, hail the Word made flesh,
   The Babe, the son of Mary!

3 So bring him incense, gold and myrrh,
   Come, peasant, king, to own him.
   The King of kings salvation brings:
   Let loving hearts enthrone him.
   Raise, raise the song on high!
   The Virgin sings her lullaby:
   Joy, joy, for Christ is born,
   The Babe, the son of Mary!

ANNUNCIATION TO THE SHEPHERDS
Nicolaes Berchem 1620–1683

WHILE SHEPHERDS WATCHED THEIR FLOCKS

ANON. (ENGLISH 16th CENT.)

WORDS ANON. (17th CENT.)

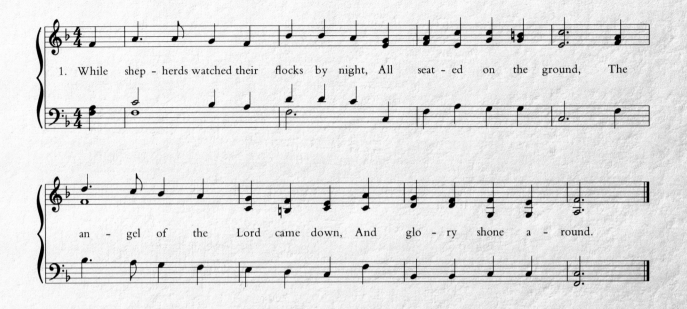

1. While shep-herds watched their flocks by night, All seat-ed on the ground, The
an-gel of the Lord came down, And glo-ry shone a-round.

2 'Fear not,' said he (for mighty dread
Had seized their troubled mind),
'Glad tidings of great joy I bring
To you and all mankind.

3 'To you in David's town this day
Is born of David's line
The Saviour, who is Christ the Lord:
And this shall be the sign:

4 'The heavenly Babe you there shall find
To human view displayed,
All meanly wrapped in swathing bands,
And in a manger laid.'

5 Thus spake the seraph; and forthwith
Appeared a shining throng
Of angels, praising God, who thus
Addressed their joyful song:

6 'All glory be to God on high,
And to the earth be peace;
Good will henceforth from heaven to men
Begin and never cease.'

WE WISH YOU A MERRY CHRISTMAS

ENGLISH TRADITIONAL

WORDS ENGLISH TRADITIONAL

1. We wish you a mer-ry Christ-mas, We wish you a mer-ry Christ-mas, We wish you a mer-ry Christ-mas, And a hap-py new year! Glad ti-dings we bring to you and your kin, We wish you a mer-ry Christ-mas, And a hap-py new year!

2 Now bring us some figgy pudding,
Now bring us some figgy pudding,
Now bring us some figgy pudding,
And bring it us here!

3 O we won't go until we've got some,
No, we won't go until we've got some,
We won't go until we've got some,
So give it us here!

4 O we all like figgy pudding,
Yes, we all like figgy pudding,
We all like figgy pudding,
So bring it out here!

A CAROL
Lawrence Alma-Tadema 1852–1909

ANNUNCIATION TO THE SHEPHERDS
manuscript

Acknowledgements

AKG: THE ARTS AND
HISTORY PICTURE LIBRARY

Pages: 7, 36, 45, 56, 59, 70, 78,

CHRISTIE'S COLOUR LIBRARY

Pages: 26, 32, 42, 61, 76, 87

ART RESOURCE

Pages : 6, 30, 34, 41

PICTUREPOINT

Pages: 8, 69

THE BRIDGEMAN ART LIBRARY

Pages: 10, 13, 14, 17, 19,
20, 23, 25, 29, 39, 46, 49, 51, 52,
62, 65, 66, 75, 81, 82, 84, 88

SOTHEBY'S
TRANSPARENCY LIBRARY

Page: 72

THE SLIDE FILE

Pages: 6, 7